T0132199

PauLey Mac

Written and Illustrated by

DARLENE ROMANSKI - STALMACH

AuthorHouse™
1663 Liberty Drive
Bloomington, IN 47403
www.authorhouse.com
Phone: 1 (800) 839-8640

© 2018 Darlene Romanski - Stalmach. All rights reserved.

No part of this publication may be reproduced in whole or in part, or stored in a retrieval system, or transmitted in any format or by any means, electronic, mechanical, photocopying, recording or otherwise, without written permission. For information regarding permission please contact the Author.

Text and Illustrations © 2017 by Darlene Romanski - Stalmach.

Published by AuthorHouse 10/03/2018

ISBN: 978-1-5462-6296-1 (sc)
ISBN: 978-1-5462-6295-4 (e)

Library of Congress Control Number: 2018911865

Print information available on the last page.

Any people depicted in stock imagery provided by Getty Images are models, and such images are being used for illustrative purposes only. Certain stock imagery © Getty Images.

This book is printed on acid-free paper.

Because of the dynamic nature of the Internet, any web addresses or links contained in this book may have changed since publication and may no longer be valid. The views expressed in this work are solely those of the author and do not necessarily reflect the views of the publisher, and the publisher hereby disclaims any responsibility for them.

authorHOUSE®

Contents

CHAPTER 1

THE WITCH

CRASH! Another soccer ball lost through a now shattered window. But not just any window. This was the window of the street's ominous, haunted house. The house that no child ever had the guts to enter or go near, especially on a dark, blustery night. The group of young boys scattered in every direction except for the new boy in the neighborhood who was unaware of *The House*.

Pauley Mac moved into the area the week before and was trying to make friends by showing off his kick ball skills. He could kick hard and far. Now, there was no doubt. Being the new kid on the block, Pauley did not know about *The House*. When all the other boys had scattered, he stood for a moment assessing the trouble he was already in. A lace curtain parted and elderly eyes assessed him back before he ran home. He failed to tell either of his parents about the ordeal.

"Why don't we just go up to the lady who lives in the house and ask her for our ball back?" Pauley asked the neighbor kids the next morning. He was surprised at the response he received. "Because she's a witch! She'll cast a spell on you!"

"Witches are only in Massachusetts," replied Pauley. "They keep them there so they can burn them for entertainment when the lights go out or when they have nothing better to do. I know. I read about it."

"Kids who tried to get their ball back before never came out of her house. They are probably still in there. Maybe she ate them but there's never been a trace. If you go in you won't come out," said Mal as he bit into his third lollipop.

Mal was a year or two older than Pauley according to Pauley's calculations. He was a bit taller than most of the other boys he was getting to know and did most of the talking. That alone made him the leader and the one boy that the others seemed to listen to the most. This was the boy who may stand in the way of Pauley being in charge of this new group of boys. This is the boy he would have to impress.

"She's just an old lady. I saw her look out the window when you all ran scared. She didn't even come out of the house to yell at me. She's not so scary," argued Pauley.

"Yeah! Well, why don't you go over and get our ball back then?"

This was a chance to prove himself to the other boys. It seemed like the right idea. If he could manage this he would surely capture every boy's respect and be the leader of the pack.

He'd do it!

First, he had to gain the courage. The courage that had quickly faded when he dreamed of the old lady with a fork and knife chasing him around a table in a large kitchen.

At breakfast Mum asked, "Did you sleep okay last night? I thought I heard you stirring in your sleep several times." Brother added, "You were yelling, too, but I couldn't make out what you were yelling about. Must have been a nightmare. You kept me awake, though. Now you owe me."

Paul made a funny face at his brother and was scolded by Mum to leave him alone. Pauley felt that Mum always favored his brother because he was a couple years younger. Dad was usually on Pauley's side though.

"Mum, the boys think that a witch lives in the ugly, green house down the road and I saw an old woman look out the window. Are witches real?"

"No such thing as a witch."

"Yes, there is! I read about it," Pauley argued. "What I meant was, are there witches around here?"

"There are women who may think they are witches. They read about spells they can cast and like to dress differently. I doubt they could ever really do anything like change you into a mouse. I don't believe that. That's just stories."

"Mum, people didn't just make this up. If everybody says the same things about them, then it must be kind of true. Maybe we just don't know. Like, we don't really know about aliens."

"Hmmmm. Sounds as if I've read you too many fairy tales."

Pauley decided he'd ask the boys for more information before he would retrieve the ball. He dressed quickly and ran outside. Seeing no one out yet, he walked to the house and stood outside looking at the broken window. The old lady had not come to his house to claim he had broken it. He didn't know how to pay for the window so that was a good thing. A voice behind him made him jump. "Scared to get the ball?" Mal asked teasingly.

"No!"

"Then, go do it. I dare ya. I double dog dare ya!"

Oh! The dreaded dare. He'd have to do it now or everyone would think he was chicken.

Pauley walked slowly across the street. He was half way when he looked back to see some kids, both boys and girls, gathering in a group to watch. He knew this was big. This was the moment. But why did he feel so nervous? He slowly walked up the creaking steps. They seemed so loud. He walked across the slanted porch noticing how badly the house needed a paint job. Maybe that's what he could do to pay for the broken window. He turned around to look at even more kids watching him. They were whispering amongst themselves and pointing. Pauley took a big gulp. His arm felt heavy as he lifted it to the grimy door knocker. Another gulp, then three loud knocks. He held his breath and closed his eyes. What if what the boys were saying is true. Would this be the moment that he may never see his family again. He might even miss his little brother. No one came to the door. He turned to the crowd and shrugged his shoulders.

"Again! Again! Again!" they chanted.

Pauley, more confidently, knocked on the door again. No answer. He walked back across the porch and down the creaky steps, across the street to the crowd of children.

"She's not there. And, I'm still here. Ha!"

"PAAAUUUULLLEEY" came Mums yell to go home. And Paul left feeling like a hero.

Pauley entered the living room where Mum was seated with a guest. So, Mum was making new friends, too. That's good for her. "Paul, this is Ms. Blackmore. She claims that you had kicked a soccer ball through her downstairs, front window and would like to know how you are going to pay for it. Did you do this without telling me or your father?"

THE WITCH WAS SITTING IN *HIS* LIVING ROOM! That's why she wasn't home. Furthermore, Mum now knew about the broken window he thought he had gotten away with.

"GGGood DDDay. I don't h have any m money."

"You can work it off, boy," was the reply. "I'll expect you tomorrow." The old woman seemed to have a gleam in her eye. What did that mean? Pauley's dog, Prince, was growling softly in the corner. It must be a sign that she's evil, thought Pauley. Prince doesn't growl unless there's trouble.

The old woman stood up to leave. "Don't bring that dog with you. My cat won't like him."

Don't all witches have cats? This was NOT good.

The door closed softly behind the woman and Pauley thought he heard a strange laugh. He didn't like this. He didn't like this at all.

"How could you break a window and not tell us?" yelled Mum. "This is how I have to meet the new neighbors, by you doing something like this? How could you not tell? Did you think you would get away with this? Go to your room and wait until your father gets home."

Pauley wasn't really worried about what Dad would say or do. He could only think about what the boys had told him, the gleam in the woman's eye, the fact that she had a cat, and how her laugh sounded when she left the house. How did she know where he lived anyway? There were too many coincidences. He did not want to go to that house. He had bad feelings.

Dad arrived home around 6:00 tired and ready to sit down, read the newspaper, and do the crossword puzzle before dinner. He was not in the mood to hear that Pauley had gotten himself into trouble in the new neighborhood already, but Mum was upset and told all. "Your son busted a window and didn't tell us. I met the neighbor under bad circumstances. He was not being honest. He should have told us. You need to do something."

"How come he's always 'your son' when he gets into trouble?" questioned Dad. What window did he break? When did all this happen?"

Dad reluctantly put the newspaper down, took a long look at his distressed wife, and walked up the thirteen steps that led to Pauley's bedroom. A sign on the door read 'YOU CAN NOT COME IN AND I MEAN IT! IF YOU WANT TO COME IN YOU HAVE TO PAY 50 CENTS. SLIDE IT UNDER THE DOOR OR I WILL NOT TALK TO YOU.'

The door was locked. "Paul, open up this door at once!"

No answer.

"Paul, open up this door or I will break it down."

No answer.

Okay, thought Dad. I can play this game. Dad got a piece of paper and a marker. He taped a note to the bathroom door and one to the kitchen door which read, YOU CAN NOT COME IN UNTIL YOU TALK TO YOUR WONDERFUL, FABULOUS, BUT UPSET PARENTS. YOU MAY NOT LEAVE THIS HOUSE UNTIL YOU HAVE SPOKEN THE TRUTH. Then he quietly went back to his favorite chair in the house to resume reading the news. "Well, did you talk to him?" "No, he'll come to us when he's either got to pee or he gets good and hungry. Let's make his favorite dish for dinner and see what happens then."

Just then, brother Mike came in from playing. His hands and little face were very dirty.

Mom said, "Mike, go wash up for dinner."

"What are we having?"

"Grilled cheese and soup."

"I don't like girl cheese. Why can't we ever have boy cheese sandwiches?" he yelled as he ascended the steps. Then, "Mum! I can't go into the bathroom! Pauley says the note says so."

"Yes, you can!"

"I pooped in the neighbor's yard," sobbed Mike.

Dad put his paper down and went upstairs. "What are you yelling about?"

"I did it! I pooped in the neighbor's yard. Their dog kept coming into our yard to poop, so I pooped in theirs. See how they like getting their shoes yucky. There! The sign says I have to tell the truth, so I did." And with that, Michael began to cry again.

"The sign was meant for your brother, not you." Dad grabbed Pauley's arm and they went into his bedroom. "You didn't tell your mother or I about the broken window. Now, you better start at the beginning and tell me everything. And it better be the truth."

"It wasn't really my fault, Dad. I really didn't kick it hard, but the wind must have blown it into the window. So, that's not really my fault. That's an act of God. Her window must have been loose or already cracked or something, because I can't kick that hard. Honest."

"'This woman, our new neighbor, saw you kick the ball that broke her window and wants you to pay for it. I think that's fair. So, son, how do you think you can do that?"

"I'm broke at the moment. But when I get money for my birthday or Christmas I can pay her."

"That's a long time away, Pauley, and you won't get enough anyway. I think you should work it off. Her house needs some fixer-upping and you can help her with chores."

"I'm not going to her house," decided Pauley and crossed his arms over his chest.

"Yes, you are. And you can start tomorrow morning."

"NO, I WON'T GO!"

"Are you talking back to me?"

"I am not talking back to you, I am face talking you."

"You will start tomorrow. Mum will take you to her house and the three of you will find out what she thinks would be suitable."

"I'm not going. She's a witch!"

"Don't be silly. Witches aren't real."

"Oh, yes they are, Dad. We pledge them every day at school. 'and to the public where witches stand, one nation, under God, invisible...'

"Look, I'm not going to argue with you anymore. You can stay in your room until morning with no dinner because you didn't come to me or Mum about that broken window." Dad stood up and walked to the doorway. He was just about out of the door when Pauley hollered, "YOU FORGOT TO LEAVE MY 50 CENTS. PUT IT TOWARDS THE WINDOW!"

Dad went downstairs and told Mum about their conversation. "What's all this about the old lady being a witch? Where did that come from?"

Mum replied, "I guess he got that from the neighborhood kids putting silly things in his head. You know, trying to break the new kid in."

"Well, I told him no dinner tonight. He can go without for his behavior. I'm not taking any of this sassing. If I would have sassed my dad, I'd have gotten a bar of soap in my mouth. Let him go hungry and learn a lesson."

Around bed time, however, Mum went upstairs to check on her son and found him reading a comic book. She had brought a sandwich and a glass of water with her just in case he was awake. "Mum, did you know water is an invisible drink?" Mum sat on the side of the bed while Pauley hungrily ate his sandwich. He was very grateful that his mum brought him something to eat. "My stomach was too loud and I couldn't go to sleep. Thank you, Mum, for making me food so I won't die."

The next day, Pauley took a half - used gallon of paint and an old brush out of Dad's shed and proceeded to the 'witches' house. He tried to be very quiet so she wouldn't know he was there. He could paint the outside of her house and she'd never see him. The other kids would see him, though, and think he was very brave. He found a stick to open the lid of the paint. So far, so good, except for the small splash on his pants. Oh well, Mum could get that out with Tide. The commercial said it tackled the toughest laundry challenges. Pauley painted the front of the house for what seemed to him a long time. The paint was nearly gone, but there was so much of the house left to do. Where would he get more paint to finish? He was supposed to be paying his debt, not spending money he didn't have to get paint to do it. This wasn't fair. Oh well. If the paint can was empty, then he must be finished too. Time to play!

"PAAAUUUULLLEEY" came Mums yell a while later. 'What does she want now', he thought, but he dutifully ran home. "Hi, Mum. What do ya need?" Then, he saw her. The witch was sitting in his living room again and somehow she looked meaner than ever. Mum's voice was very tense when she asked, "Did you do some painting this morning?"

"Yes!" Pauley answered proudly. "I began bright and early so you would be proud of me. I've worked my way through all the paint in the can and I only got a little on me so you wouldn't be mad at me. There's nothing left so I am finished. Aren't you proud of me?" And he stood tall and let out a wide smile.

The old lady was furious, however. "YOU painted MY house PURPLE! YOU didn't even come to ME and ASK me what I needed done. And it WOULDN'T have been THAT! I don't want MY house painted by some LITTLE KID! YOU didn't even PICK UP the MESS YOU LEFT! This is WORSE than before and I am going to CALL THE POLICE!"

"WAIT, PLEASE! I assure you that won't be necessary. I am very sure that we can straighten this out somehow, please!" Pauley never heard mum sound like this before. It was as if she was about to cry.

"You don't like the pretty job I did?" he interrupted confused. *He* thought he did a very nice job and was so careful not to spill the paint like he usually spilled his milk. In fact, he was very proud of the job he did. It wasn't his fault Dad didn't have enough paint in the shed to finish the whole house. Besides, he was afraid to climb up a ladder if he had to, so, to him, it all worked out fine.

"Little boys should be seen and not heard," said Ms. Blackmore.

"I AM NOT A LITTLE BOY!" shouted Pauley. "AND I DID MY BEST JOB!"

"PAULEY! Go to your room."

This was not fair! He worked so hard! How could she take the witches side?

"NO! YOU ARE NOT THE BOSS. DADDY IS. CUZ HE HAS HAIR IN HIS ARMPITS."

Mom stood up. And she was angry! GO TO YOUR ROOM, NOW!

This time something told Pauley he had better.

"JUST WAIT TIL YOUR FATHER GETS HOME, YOUNG MAN!"

Well, at least Mum didn't think he was a 'little' boy.

"When my husband gets home, I assure you, we will work this out. There is no need to involve the police. My husband will know what to do."

"He'd better know what to do and he'd better get control of that kid of yours. Good day!"

Mum peeked out the window as Ms. Blackmore stomped off. She was shocked once again at the partially painted purple house her son was responsible for. What a hideous sight! She sat down unnerved by the situation.

Dad came home at his usual time of 6:00 ready to relax with his newspaper and some TV, but was greeted at the door by his frantic wife instead. "Do you know what your son did today?"

"Uh oh."

"Well, I don't even need to tell you. You can look across the street for yourself."

Dad opened the door and stood in the doorway gazing at Ms. Blackmore's house across the street while mum filled him in on the situation. He didn't say anything for a while. Then, "I suppose Paul is upstairs?"

"He's in his room."

Dad ascended the stairs two at a time. He paused outside of Pauley's bedroom door and ripped the sign down before entering his room. "Do you want to explain to me what happened?"

"No." "Let's try this again. "You BETTER explain to me what happened."

Pauley began to cry. He'd better make this good or a spanking might follow. I wanted to (sniff) make everyone proud of me (sniff). So, I helped by doing chores to pay my way for the broken window (sniff). But she didn't like purple paint and I didn't know it. (sob) Now I have to start all over again and I don't know even what her favorite color is." Some crying time. "I worked all morning (sniff) and I was sweating, too. I used the whole can and I thought EVERYBODY likes purple. It's Grace Griffin's favorite color at school. And her house really needed painting. And now it looks a little good, I think. And I didn't get much paint on me. And I didn't even spill it. And I was quiet and everything so I didn't bother anybody. I'm so happy I was good."

Dad sat on the edge of Pauley's bed pondering all this. Part of him wanted to kind of laugh at the situation, but he knew he had to be stern. "The trouble is, son, that you didn't ask. You took it upon yourself with no adult supervision. You can't do that. You must always ask. If you would have done so, this probably wouldn't have happened. I want you to think about that. And never raise your voice to your mother again. Do you hear me?"

"Are you gonna clobber me now, Dad, or after I hear you?"

"I'm going to think about your punishment because I'm not happy with you. Right now, you're grounded, then we'll see what else. Tomorrow morning, I'm taking you across the street to Ms. Blackmore's myself and we will sit down and figure this mess out. You're lucky she didn't call the police."

"Gee, Dad. Would they put me in jail?"

"Could be."

"And I'd only get bread and water?"

"Probably."

"Dad? Did you know water is an invisible drink?"

"Good night, son."

The next morning, Dad made sure Pauley looked very neat and clean before going to Ms. Blackmore's.

"It isn't a school day, Dad. Why do I have to get all clean and everything?"

"It's always good policy to look representable when you're in trouble."

"Why don't you get dressed up when Mum's mad at you?"

"Let's go."

Pauley hesitated. "Dad, the guys all say she's a witch. We have to be really careful or we might not ever come home again."

"Come on, Paul. Quit hesitating. She's not a witch. And don't call her that. EVER! Understand?"

Dad dragged Pauley by the hand across the street to Ms. Blackmore's. There were several kids at the playground, but, so far, they didn't seem to notice. Dad stopped to pick up the discarded paint can and brush and was about to ask Pauley to run them home, but somehow knew his son may not come back, so just left them on the sidewalk. They climbed the creaky steps, walked across the slanted porch and knocked. And there she was. Dressed in black. Pauley was scared! This is the end, he thought. "Enter", she said. Who says 'enter'? It's always 'Come in', 'How are ya', 'Good day', or something to that effect. Pauley took a large swallow. Dad said, "Good morning, Ms. Blackmore. How are you today?" He didn't wait for an answer as if he knew it wasn't going to be a good one. "My son and I have come over to rectify yesterday's situation. We hope to come to a mutual conclusion for his actions."

"And get my ball back", added Pauley.

"Be quiet and don't talk unless we ask you a question. Got it?"

"Yes, Dad."

"Pauley here will do whatever odd jobs you ask him to do to help pay for the damages."

"I need my window replaced and my entire house painted."

"I will call to have estimates taken for the paint job. I know a man who can fix the window. I've already talked to him and he will be over later this afternoon, if that is alright. Now, what kind of work can my son do for you?"

"Step into my kitchen so we are away from this draft from the window."

Pauley's mind began to churn. Didn't the witch in Hansel and Gretel have a kitchen? Isn't that where she was going to bake Gretel? He began to sweat. He didn't want to go into her kitchen, but Dad was pulling his arm. On her stove was a large, bubbling pot. She picked up a large, wooden spoon and began to stir the contents. To Pauley, it did not smell good. Witches had brews they made with large pots. What could be in it? He felt his knees going weak. She certainly looked like a witch today all dressed in black. Things were adding up very quickly. She *had* to be a witch! But, just then, a black cat jumped upon the cupboard next to the pot and that was IT! "AAAWWWWW!" yelled Pauley as he let go of Dad's sweaty hand, ran across the living room and out the front door, down the creaky steps, tripped on the paint can skinning his knees, and ran across the street without stopping all the way to his house, but leaving a puddle on the old woman's kitchen floor first.

"I DON'T WANT THAT BOY IN MY HOUSE OR NEAR MY HOUSE EVER AGAIN!" she screamed while handing Dad a roll of paper towels.

"I assure you, Ms. Blackmore, that all damages to your home will be taken care of." Dad quietly turned and walked out of the house - after cleaning up the pee.

"WHERE'S PAUL? I'm gonna kill 'em", shouted Dad when he got home.

Mother just pointed upstairs.

Dad threw open Pauley's bedroom door but Pauley had already taken cover under his bed.

"COME OUT OF THERE!" yelled Dad.

"I'm sorry, Dad! I couldn't help it! I've never been this age before!" But Pauley knew he better stay put or a spanking was going to happen for sure.

"Paul, come out!"

"No! You can't hit me or your hand will get all wet!"

Dad moved the bed, but Pauley held on to the bedsprings and slid with it. He was determined not to come out from under the bed until he was sure his parents had calmed down, even if it took days.

Sometime much later, Pauley crawled out from under the bed. He knew it was late enough where Dad had already gone to bed. He would not see Dad again until after work the next day. Dad did most of the hitting, so he was safe until six. He had bloody knees and elbows from falling over the paint can in his haste to get away from the witches' house and a tear stained face.

"Mum?" he called. He walked into the kitchen where Mum was sitting at the table with a cup of tea.

"Oh, Pauley. Look at you. Come here."

"Are you gonna hit me?"

"No, I'm going to clean you up a bit."

Pauley came over to Mum and she lifted him up on the counter. She took a washcloth from the drawer and wet it with warm, soapy water and began to gently clean his face, elbows and knees.

"OOOOOwwwww! Are you gonna put a boo boo sticker on it?" "Yes, of course. Now hold still. Pauley, we need to talk about being more polite when we have guests." "Oh, I already know about that, Mummy. When we say something nice, even if we don't mean it at all, that's being polite, right?"

"Ummm. Listen, when Ms. Blackmore was here, you were disrespectful. You should never raise your voice to any adult. Your actions the last few days have gotten you into a lot of trouble and you have consequences. You will be grounded for two weeks and you will be doing a lot of chores around the house to earn money to pay for your damages. You will begin right away."

"You mean I don't have to go to *her house* to do chores?"

"That's right. She doesn't want you near her house. You are never to go there again."

"Yippee! I'm so happy to be alive! I'll do anything!"

Chapter 2

The Haircut

Prince was a great dog. He followed the boys wherever they went and looked after them. He was the kind of dog that seemed to understand everything that was said and tilted his head as he listened. He was a fast runner. Pauley and Mike believed he was better than Lassie.

One rainy day, Prince took off after a rabbit. He didn't listen as the boys called for him to come back and had taken off into the woods. "We gotta save him! There are wolves and spooky things in the woods that'll get him!" The boys ran outside towards the woods in the direction of their dog. They didn't notice how soft the ground was or how their shoes sank into the mud at every step. They just had to save Prince. After all, Prince would have saved them, wouldn't he?

"PRINCE! PRINCE!" they called but Prince wasn't coming back. "We'll keep looking. I bet he went down by the railroad tracks. Once I saw a rabbit on the tracks. He's probably looking for it. Let's go!"

The boys were now wet and muddy, but still did not find their dog.

"I'm mad at Prince. He should have come when we called him. Let's go home. I'm cold."

"Yeah, dumb dog."

And so they did, after they put pennies on the tracks and waited for the next train to come by and run them over.

When they finally reached home, Prince was waiting by the back door. His fur was wet and matted down with mud which made him look a little skinnier and a bit funnier than usual.

"We better give him a bath before Mum sees him. She might be mad if he's like this and won't let him in the house. But she would be all happy if Prince was clean," reasoned Pauley.

Pauley picked Prince up and the two boys made their way to the bathroom after Mike went into Dad's shed to get a bucket and the dog soap.

"What are you boys up to?" called Mum from the kitchen where she was putting a salad together for lunch.

"Nothing. Just going upstairs," they called back.

"Alright. Lunch will be ready in just a bit. Wash up, please."

"We will."

They filled the tub with water and placed the wiggly dog into the tub. The dog shook and mud splattered all over the bathroom. This made the boys giggle as they got sprayed.

"I wonder what Prince would look like with short hair," said Pauley.

"Let's give him a haircut and see," said Mike.

"No. We can't. We're not allowed to use Dad's razor. I did that once and got into *big* trouble."

"We can use scissors. We're allowed to use those."

"Okay! Go get 'em!"

Mike was back in a flash with the scissors from Mum's sewing basket. Pauley scolded him for not carrying them properly. He loved showing his authority to his younger brother. The boys began to cut off Prince's beautiful, but muddy fur.

"He's gonna look really good and he's gonna be a lot cooler with a haircut."

Chop, chop, chop. They put the fur into the bucket as they cut.

"Dad said I needed a haircut. If you cut my hair, Pauley, it would save Dad some money and he could put it towards the witches' house."

"Yeah, and he said he didn't have any time this week to go to the barber's, so we would save him time AND money. And Dad says time is precious. Come here and I'll cut yours, then you can cut mine."

Pauley placed a towel around Mike's shoulders. "Just like a real barber," he bragged. He cut Mike's hair as close to his head as he could, feeling very sure his parents would be so happy at what he was doing. They were very quiet and concentrated on their efforts.

"What are the boys doing? I haven't seen much of them this morning," asked Dad.

"Oh, they are upstairs washing up for lunch. Seems like they've been up there awhile, though. I better go up and check. Lunch is ready."

Mum climbed up the steps. "Boys, time for lunch."

Silence.

"Boys! Come on down for lunch."

Silence.

Mum opened the door to the bathroom. Mud was sprayed on the walls from Prince who was still shaking off water. The brown and white fur from his back and the top of his head was cut off and fur was floating in the tub. Wet, muddy clothes were draped on the towel rack and a small, dirty pool of water formed underneath. Multiple towels were lying on the bathroom floor, soaked. Muddy, wet, ruined shoes were on the toilet seat. A bucket of a mixture of hair and fur was between the boys. Michael had a haircut that had little tufts of hair sticking up and bald spots in other places.

"UUUUUUH! DAD! HELP!"

Dad took the steps three at a time. "What is it?" And then he saw, too. Mum began to cry.

"Look, Mike, Mum is so happy she's crying!" beamed Pauley.

"My bathroom! Your head! Look at this mess! And It's right before school pictures!"

"Sorry we didn't have time to do *my* haircut."

Dad picked up the dog and quickly put him outside. Then, he placed both boys in the shower until the caked-on mud came off. He dried them and carried them both to their room wrapped in clean towels while mum began to wipe up mud from floors and walls.

"What the **ll were you thinking? I've never seen a bigger mess! Why would you cut off your brother's hair?" fumed Dad.

"YOU CUSSED!" they both chanted at the same time.

But dad did not look happy. In fact, he looked a little scary.

"I saved you time and money," answered a confused Pauley.

"We gave Prince a bath cuz he was all muddy," said Mike.

"You two made a huge mess! That's what you did. A MESS! And you made your Mum cry. Well, I've never seen anything like this. Stay in your room and don't move." Dad left the boys to go help his wife clean up the bathroom.

"The tub is clogged. There's even hair and fur in the toilet. I just don't even know where to begin to clean up this mess."

"I'll take the towels down and put them in the washer to soak," said Dad.

They cleaned the bathroom for hours before it was normal, delaying lunch.

"Let's eat. I'm starved," said Dad.

"What about the boys?" asked Mum.

"Leave them in their rooms. I don't even want to look at them right now. I might lose my temper."

But, Pauley was upstairs, mad. "All this WORK, all this TROUBLE. We gave Prince a bath, and you got a haircut, and what THANKS do WE get? NOTHING! We saved Prince's life from the wolves. NO ONE 'preciates what we did. I don't get it. And I'm hungry and kids can DIE without food."

That made Mike begin to cry. "I don't want to die. I'm too young to die!"

Dad went up to the boy's bedroom later that evening. He sat on the edge of the bed and told the boys to explain what they were doing.

"We wanted to help you. We saved our dog's life from the wolves. We didn't want a dead dog. And Mike got a haircut, but I didn't even get a chance to finish it, or you would have liked it better. And we would have cleaned up, but there wasn't enough time cuz Mum was too quick. We tried hard, though, cuz we love you soooooo much. And we really are nice boys. It's all Prince's fault anyway cuz he ran off after that rabbit and didn't come back when we called him. And we really need to eat or we won't grow right."

Dad sat quietly while Pauley rambled on and on. Then he heard Mum scream again. "THERE'S A DEAD RABBIT BY THE BACK DOOR!"

CHAPTER 3

MEMAW'S HOUSE

"Memaw!" Pauley and Mike ran through the door to find their grandmother in the kitchen making homemade soup. She always seemed to be cooking in front of the stove with her faded, flowered, pink apron on. There was no place like Memaw's. The house smelled of her, and her of it. She kept bananas in the middle drawer on the right-hand side and Pauley always helped himself, first thing. He knew she always left them there especially for him. Memaw bent down to give her grandsons a big, bear hug and a kiss on the forehead. "That's quite a haircut, Mike," she exclaimed looking curiously at Mum.

"Long story," she replied. "Thanks for keeping them for the weekend. I just truly feel exhausted and need to rest." Memaw led Mum to a kitchen chair and put on the tea pot so they could talk as the boys ran outside to find the toys that were kept there. "They just wear me down. I'm trying to be a good mum, but why didn't I see Pauley painting that house, or notice that he had a frog in the dryer. And then the whole dog and haircut thing! Thanks so much for having them."

"You know the old saying – 'boys will be boys'. You just get a little rest this weekend and you'll be fine. Don't worry about a thing."

Mum finished her tea and checked on the boys to say goodbye. Kisses all around. "If you need anything, or if they give you any trouble, don't hesitate to call me."

"Oh, they'll be fine. Don't worry. Now, off with ya."

Memaw sat down on the picnic table to watch the boys play with their toys. They were growing so fast! Pauley looked so much like his dad with his big eyes and long lashes. He would break the girls' hearts one day.

"Well, it's great to have you boys here," said Memaw.

"We're glad to be here, too. Our Mum likes it when we're out of the house so she can have company over and don't get a headache," replied Pauley.

Memaw smiled at his honesty. "Let's all go in and have a sandwich and a bowl of soup. Run along and wash your hands."

The boys did exactly as they were told, but leaving behind a dirty sink with the water slightly running and a muddy towel on the bathroom floor.

"Well, here we are!"

"This is so nice to have your company. What kind of a sandwich would you like? We have egg salad, tuna, or peanut butter and jelly."

"I want tuna," answered Mike.

"I would like peanut butter and jelly and brown cow milk, please," answered Pauley.

"I want brown cow milk, too," said Mike.

"Don't say 'want', corrected Pauley to his younger brother. "Say, 'I would like'. You have to have manners here. Dad said so."

"Manners are important in life. You should always use them. They can get you far and they may get you out of trouble someday," said Memaw.

"I use them, but I still get in trouble," replied Pauley.

"Hmmm. Well, Pauley, you're in luck because I just made home-made strawberry jelly. It's going to taste really good on your sandwich."

Pauley gave a frown to his grandmother. "Where did you get the jellyfish? They sting, ya know."

"What jellyfish?"

"The jellyfish you made the jelly from. How do you know which kind of jellyfish makes strawberry?"

"Pauley, jelly doesn't come from a jellyfish."

"Yes, it does! Sponge Bob said so!"

"No, it comes from fruit."

"No, it doesn't!"

"Yes, that's why we have strawberry, peach, grape..."

"SPONGE BOB SAYS SO AND HE NEVER LIES!"

It now occurred to Memaw that this may, indeed, be a very long weekend.

After lunch, Memaw took the boys for a walk to a creek near her house. The boys played in the cool water, skipped stones, and wrote with a long stick in the wet dirt. Mike wrote; 'Grace ♥ Pauley'.

"Hey, I don't ever want to see you do THAT again!" yelled Pauley. "Okay, close your eyes!" came the reply. "Silence, you peasant!" yelled Pauley, and the bickering went back and forth, so Memaw said it was time to leave.

That evening, the trio watched television and ate popcorn. Memaw knew how to make colored popcorn 'the old-fashioned way'. The boys loved to watch it pop in the large kettle with the clear lid. They liked picking out the color the popcorn would be from the little food coloring containers. And then, they'd gobble it down.

"Do you boys still take baths together?"

"NO!!!! We're way too old for that! That ended when Michael's butt blew bubbles all the time!"

"Okay, I wasn't sure. But, we better start getting ready for bed. You two need a bath after swimming in the creek. The towels are in the linen closet. While you're getting ready for bed, I'll get ready, too."

"You can go first, Mike."

"Wow, thanks! I never get to go first."

It wasn't that Pauley was being kind. He just figured if Mike took his bath first, he could play as long as he wanted in the tub. While Pauley was bathing, Mike went to find Memaw. She was in her bathroom putting bobby pin curls in her hair. He saw a jar on a shelf near the sink that had her false teeth in it. He stared and stared at the jar before exclaiming, "The tooth fairy is never going to believe this!" Memaw laughed loudly. "Those are dentures, Mike." Mike asked, "Is there a denture fairy?" Memaw laughed and said they should get Pauley out of the tub before he shrivels like a prune and both boys needed to get to bed.

"Come on, Pauley, you'll turn into a prune. Out of the tub and I'll tell you boys a story." Pauley loved Memaw's stories and was ready in a flash. The only bad part about staying at Memaw's is that they had to share a bed. Mike kicked a lot in his sleep and kept Pauley awake all night. Pauley was complaining about the sleeping arrangements and said he would sleep downstairs on the couch. Memaw said absolutely not. She felt better with everyone upstairs on the same floor and that was that.

"Maybe Cain and Abel would not have killed each other if they had their own rooms," said Pauley.

"Hush, and listen to a story. Now, what kind of story do you like? Or, do you like nursery rhymes; little girls are made of sugar and spice and everything nice...." "NO, THEY'RE NOT! They are made of blood and bones..." Memaw sighed. She was very tired after just one day of having the boys. She wondered how she had done it when her kids were little.

About 2:00 a.m. she was awakened. The boys sounded a bit frantic. She grabbed her bathrobe and rushed to their room to see what was the matter.

"There's a monster under the bed!" shouted Mike as he sat in the middle of the bed and hugged the pillow close to himself.

"No, there's not. There is no such thing as monsters. Look, your big brother isn't afraid. You just had a bad dream." Memaw flicked the lights on.

"NO! It was REAL!" sobbed Mike.

+ Pauley crawled out of bed, got down on the floor and looked under the bed. "There's nothing under here except a dead bug, a sock, and a bobby pin. No monster. Can we go back to sleep now?"

As Mike shook off his dream he grew brave enough to look under the bed, too. "Can we sleep with the light on, Memaw?"

"Of course, if it makes you feel better."

Oh, how Pauley hated sleeping with his little brother!

The boys slept later than Memaw expected and she was glad for the little bit of quiet time that morning. She decided to surprise the boys by making bacon and pancakes- cutting the pancakes into shapes with cookie cutters. She put a bottle of water at each of their plates. It looked perfect. Soon, down the stairs they came in their pajamas and socks, sleepy-eyed. They were delighted by the pancakes, but Pauley had a problem with the water. "It's expired. It's no good. We can't drink it!"

"What do you mean? There's nothing wrong with that bottle of water."

"It says it's Spring Water, but this is summer. We can't drink it!"

Memaw quietly got up. She knew by now it was useless arguing with this boy. She got two cups, went to the sink and poured water into the cups. "Here, this is today's water. Nice and fresh," she said and watched as the boys shook their heads yes and drank the 'fresh' tap water.

"Memaw, Pauley has a girlfriend! I think girls stink!"

"Not all of them," replied Pauley.

"Is it true? You have a girlfriend, Pauley?"

"Yes! I might even be in love. She's very pretty. She has shiny, black hair."

"Ahhh! Love. You're too young to be in love. You don't even know what love is," said Memaw.

"I do too, know what it is," came Pauley's reply as Mike kept chanting "girls stink, girls stink, girls stink!"

"What is it, honey?"

"Love is when a girl puts on perfume and a boy puts on after shave and then they go out and smell each other. And then little hearts come out of you."

"How lovely!" And Memaw said she agreed.

"When is Mummy coming to get us? I miss Mummy," said Mike. "I have little hearts come out when Mummy hugs me."

"Daddy must have huge hearts come out when Mummy hugs him,"

said Pauley. "Daddy loves to hug Mummy. And kiss her too! I want to kiss Grace Griffin, but I'm afraid to."

"Mummy's coming after dinner tonight. Do you boys want to go back down to the creek and play or would you like me to take you to the zoo?"

"To the creek!" they hollered in unison.

"Alright, then, put the clothes on you wore yesterday. I washed them out and they are folded on top of the dryer. That way, the other set of clothes you brought we will change into when Mummy comes to get you later. Let's go find some old buckets and shovels we can take with us to the creek to play."

The boys did exactly as they were told and were soon ready for another creek adventure.

"Can we take the fishing poles?" asked Pauley. "Maybe we can catch our dinner and then we can earn our keep. We can eat fish and French Flies for dinner."

"Of course, we can," said Memaw laughing.

The trio piled everything into an old, rusty wagon and set off for the creek.

Once there, they decided to dig for worms to go fishing. This turned into a contest to see who could catch the longest and fattest worms. Memaw was amused how everything the boys did was a competition. She remembered how her own boys would do the same thing.

"Now, don't go to close to the edge of that dock. It might be a little deep." Memaw sat back on the blanket she had spread out with her face to the sun while the boys fished. "Catch our dinner. Make it a whopper!"

Mike and Pauley threw in their lines. Little red and white bobbers floated on the surface. It seemed like forever until they got a nibble. Pauley yanked his line in very hard. This must be 'the big one', he thought. He yanked again but the fish was either really big or the line was snagged. Dad had shown Pauley how to walk back and forth with the line held firm to help remove it from whatever it was snagged on. And this is what he did, but he was paying too much attention to the line and not to where he was going.

SPLASH! Memaw sat up straight and looked over to where her grandsons were fishing. Mike was there. Where was....there he was! Coming up out of the water covered in green mucky seaweed and mud!

"I got my hook loose!" he yelled happily. "Don't worry, Memaw, it's not deep!"

To Memaw, he looked like a slimy, green monster. She got up and made her way over to the boy as quickly as she could. "What on earth!"

Mike began to yell at Pauley, "YOU SCARED AWAY ALL THE FISH. I was just about to catch a big one and YOU made me LOOSE IT!"

"BOYS! I believe it is time to go back."

"We don't want to. We're having too much fun."

"Pauley, look at you! We need to get you out of those clothes. OH! They SMELL!"

"Can we come back?"

"Maybe next time. Let's get you back before this all dries on you. Oh! You reek!"

Michael chanted on the way back, "Pauley smells, Pauley smells...."

Memaw said the boys could run through the garden hose for a little while. She had to get all the muck off Pauley before he came into the house. Then, she made sure the boys each got another bath – Pauley first this time. She took his clothes to the washer and put her hands in the pockets to check for papers or tissues. "Ahhhhh, what's that?" She pulled the pocket out and found a half dozen worms still wiggling about. The other pocket had some sticks and pebbles. Good thing she checked first before just throwing the clothes into the washer.

After baths, it was already time for dinner. Memaw had taken a fish out of the freezer and thawed it under running hot water before the boys came downstairs to dinner. "Look! I found this in your pocket! You did catch a fish today, after all!"

"Wow! Can I eat it?"

"No. We only have one fish and three people. You can take it home with you to show Mummy and Daddy. She laughed a sly little laugh. How about pizza instead?"

"Yeah! Pizza!"

Memaw called for take-out and everyone was soon eating dinner.

"Pizza is like people. It can be big or small, thick or thin, and even stuffed like me," reasoned Pauley.

Soon after, Mummy came to pick them up. "I hope they weren't any trouble for you."

"Oh, no, none at all," lied an exhausted Memaw.

Kisses all around as they left their smiling, tired grandmother.

In the car, Pauley turned to Mummy and said, "Ya know, Memaw's pretty good with kids. Too bad she doesn't have any of her own."

Chapter 4

The Doctor Visit

The weekend with Memaw was a blast, but falling in the creek may have resulted in a stomach virus. Right before Mike's birthday, too. What if he couldn't eat cake?

"Hmm. I think you picked up a virus, Pauley. Let me feel your forehead."

"I didn't pick anything up, Mum. I didn't even have a bucket."

"Well, you have a fever and I think maybe we should visit the doctor."

"NO! I DON'T WANT TO GO TO THE DOCTOR! I DON'T WANT TO GET A SHOT!"

"If the fever doesn't break, then we will *need* to go. We'll see how you feel later, but I'm going to give him a call now."

Pauley knew he was feeling pretty sick. He made frequent trips to the bathroom to vomit. His stomach hurt and he had no appetite. Not even for cake - his favorite. Still, he was secretly glad that he didn't have to go to school today because there was going to be a spelling test and he hadn't studied for it. He couldn't even remember this week's word pattern.

After Mike left for school, with much complaining because his brother was staying home and he wasn't, Pauley climbed back in bed and soon fell back to sleep. Mum checked on him throughout the morning, feeling his forehead and taking his temperature which did not drop. When Pauley woke up Mum dressed him warmly, heated the car, buckled him in and they were off to see Dr. Robert.

"Mrs. Mac. It's good to see you. How have you been?" asked Dr. Robert.

"I'm tired. I've been up half the night cleaning puke and changing sheets. How are you?"

"Awww, the joys of parenthood," joked Dr. Robert. "I'm well, thank you for asking. And Pauley, good to see you. How are you feeling today?"

"Well, if I felt good then I wouldn't be here so I must feel bad," was the answer. "I have a tummy egg, but I'm sure I don't need a shot."

"You're getting big! What grade are you in now?"

"First grade."

"How do you like first grade?"

"We're learning about the 'Entire State Building'. And you're a mammal. My dad's a reptile because he has no hair. It's a bit tricky. If second grade is like this one then it's going to be a nightmare."

"Well, let's see. You haven't been here for a long time. I think we better do a complete physical while I have you here. Hop up on the table and let's get a look."

Pauley climbed up and took off his shoes. "I see my pig toe ate the top of my sock again." Then he sat still and quiet as the doctor took his temperature and blood pressure.

"Well, he has a fever of 101.2. Let's get a urine sample. Pauley, can you be a big boy and pee in this cup?"

"I don't have to drink it, do I?"

"Of course not," chuckled Dr. Robert.

"Then I can. I have good aim. I can hit the handle on the boy's toilet at school."

"PAUL!" corrected Mum.

"You can go into that bathroom across the hall. Only pee in the cup, now, not on the handle, please. When you are done, leave it by the sink and the nurse will get it."

"What does she want it for? That's a really stinky job. I hope you pay her lots of money."

When Pauley came back he sat back up on the table. He handed Dr. Robert the empty cup.

"I told you to pee in it. What happened?"

"There was already a toilet in there so I didn't need the cup. You can have it back."

The doctor prepared a booster shot to help him feel better and stop the vomiting. Another nurse came into the room and took a cotton ball with some smelly stuff on it and began to rub his arm.

"I DON'T WANT A SHOT, I DON'T WANT A SHOT!" yelled Pauley.

"It will only pinch for a minute," said Mum in a calming voice.

But Pauley squirmed. He tried to cover his arm with his other hand. Mum and the nurse held him still so Dr. Robert could administer the shot.

"Be a big boy, Pauley. *This will be a piece of cake.* I promise."

"I'm not crying. My eyes are sweating."

In a minute, it was all over and Pauley could show off his Batman sticker to his little brother. Pauley put his shoes back on and his coat and hat to go home.

"Would you like a toy from the treasure box or a sticker?" asked Dr. Robert.

"I would like my piece of cake," answered Pauley.

Doctor Robert just rubbed his chin, smiled and gave Pauley another sticker. Mum thanked Dr. Robert for his help then went to the reception window to pay for the appointment. Pauley watched her take out the money from her purse. "Why do we have to pay for something that doesn't feel very good?" Mum didn't answer. Pauley said nothing more. Even in the car on the way home he didn't say a word. When he got home he went straight to his room.

A little later Mike and Dad got home. Mike wanted to play with his big brother but Pauley still wasn't talking. Mike picked up some dirty socks off the bedroom floor and threw them at Pauley's face. That should make him say something for sure, thought Mike.

"LEAVE ME ALONE! DO YOU HAVE ANY IDEA WHAT I'VE BEEN THROUGH!" Pauley yelled.

Downstairs, Dad was asking mum how her day had been. "Not too bad," replied Mum. "You know it's a good day when your kid gets all the vomit in the toilet. Sick days were much more fun when I was the kid and not the adult."

At bedtime, an exhausted Mum sat on the edge of Pauley's bed and held him as she read him his favorite story, <u>Sam and the Firefly</u>. "Are you warm enough, son?" she asked.

"Who needs a warm bed when you have a warm Mummy," whispered Pauley, cuddling into his mother. "Thanks for helping me be better. When I'm too big for you to hold me, I'll hold you instead."

Kind words always make mummies feel all better.

Chapter 5

Grace Griffin

Mr. Mac was amused and surprised to hear his eldest son's latest remark as the family sat on the living room floor playing a board game Friday night. "Girls stink!" was Mike's exclamation about how he was upset when a girl in his classroom obtained a lot of attention for a sentence she wrote. Mike thought his writing was far better than *that* girls. "They just STINK!"

"Not **all** of them," Pauley replied to everyone's amazement. "The girl who sits in front of me doesn't stink."

"Who sits in front of you?" asked Mum.

"Grace Griffin and she doesn't ever stink."

What makes her so special?" asked Dad.

"She wears blue flowered panties. They're quite nice."

Mum and Dad exchanged glances and felt full of questions.

"How'd you see her panties?" asked Mike in disgust, plugging his nose.

"She bent down to pick up her pencil and I saw them.

And I see them when she climbs the steps on the sliding board. I think I might be in love. I can't stop thinking about them." Pauley made a long, deep sigh.

In a few days, Dad was called to the principal's office. An attractive woman Dad did not know from all his previous visits to school was already there.

"I'm sorry to have to call you, but we've had a little incident with Paul. This is Mrs. Griffin and she claims your son has been lifting her daughter's uniform dress up and the class has been laughing at Grace. Also, her lunch money is often missing as well as pencils, erasers, and the like. What do you know about this?"

"Well, Paul said she dropped her pencil and he saw her underclothes."

"Mr. Mac, he was caught this time using his ruler to lift up her clothing and he is deliberately knocking the pencils off her desk. He's causing a disruption to the entire class."

"Oh." Dad felt very uncomfortable.

"Poor Gracie cries every morning and doesn't want to come to school anymore. She always loved school before," said Mrs. Griffin.

Mr. Mac felt like all eyes and blame were on him. It was bringing back memories from his own school days. He felt as though he needed to have a good answer for his son and defend him, yet, another part of him was thinking about how you punish a boy for this. What could be a win - win situation?

"Well, let's call Paul in and see what he has to say," suggested the principal. He pressed the intercom to have his secretary get Pauley from his classroom. "May I have Paul Mac, please, to come to the office?" All the other children in the room went 'oooooooh', making the 'you're in trouble' noise and feeling thankful it wasn't them being called to the office instead.

Pauley stood up, glanced at his teacher for a signal to leave the room, then slowly walked the long hall to the principal's office as his teacher quieted the class.

When Pauley saw dad in the office, he knew he was in for it. "Hi, Dad," said Pauley in a faint voice. Dad didn't even smile and Pauley knew this wasn't going to be pleasant.

The principal began. "Come in, Paul, and take a seat. This is Mrs. Griffin. You know Grace, I'm sure."

"Yes, I do. Nice to meet you, Mrs. Griffin," Paul responded by standing and using his best manners as he shook Mrs. Griffin's hand.

No one seemed amused or impressed.

The principal said, "Explain what your teacher wrote on the detention notice.

"I couldn't help myself," Pauley began to sniffle. I LOVED those blue flowered panties. Sometimes they were PINK or YELLOW even! I HAD to see." A tear ran down is face. "I have her lunch money and stuff. I'll give it all back. I only wanted to *hold* her things. I wasn't gonna keep 'em. I just wanted, I don't know... I'm not a thief."

"STOP THAT BLUBBERING," hollered Dad. "You better never – EVER...."

"I won't, I won't, I promise! I'm NOT in love with her anymore."

"What are you talking about?"

"She doesn't wear flowered panties anymore. She stinks like all the other girls, only worse even! Today she wore panties that said Monday and it's Wednesday! I'm done with girls UNDERLINE FOREVER!"

Printed in the United States
By Bookmasters